MOBY

PLAY

All songs licensed by
WARNER BROS. MUSIC ITALY s.r.l. - Milano

MOBY

PLAY

10 - 7

by Richard Hall

DOWN SLOW

by Richard Hall

BODYROCK

by Richard Hall, Bobby Robinson, Gabriel M. Jackson

Rock

Rock, y'all non stop, y'all to the beat, y'all the bo-dy-rock, y'all. So let's

only Voice and Drums

rock, y'all non stop, y'all to the beat, y'all the bo-dy-rock, y'all. So let's

rock, y'all non stop, y'all to the beat, y'all the bo-dy-rock, y'all. So let's

EVERLOVING

by Richard Hall

FIND MY BABY

by Richard Hall

Moderato

only Voice and Drums
I'm gon-na find my ba-by, — whoo won't that sun go— down. I'm gon-na

find my ba - by, — whoo won't that sun go— down

I'm gon-na find my ba - by, — whoo won't that sun

18

GUITAR FLUTE AND STRING

by Richard Hall

HONEY

by Richard Hall

Moderato

When my ho-ney comes back, some-times I'm gon-na rap that jack, some-times I'll

(repeat 3 times)

get a hump in— my back, some-times I'm going o - ver here, some-times.

When my ho-ney comes back, some-times I'm gon-na rap that jack, some-times I'll

when my ho-ney comes back, some-times when my ho-ney comes back, some-times.

Bm7

When my ho-ney comes back, when my ho-ney comes back, when my ho-ney comes back,

no Drums

Sim7

when my ho-ney comes back. When my ho-ney comes back, when my ho-ney comes back,

with Drums

when my honey comes back, when my honey comes back. Way down yon-der some-times,

28

IF THINGS WERE PERFECT

by Richard Hall

Moderato

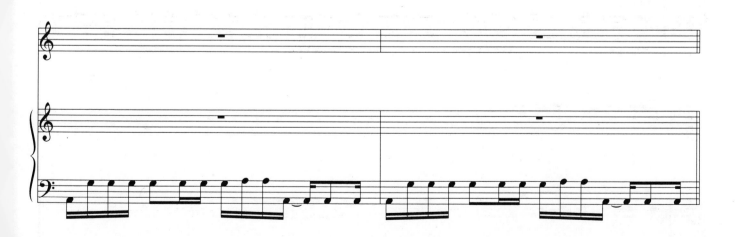

Give me sum - mer.

Give me sum - mer.

Give me sum - mer.
Give me sum - mer.
Give me sum - mer.

A5

La5

32

wrapped in cold,   late at night.
wrapped in cold,   late at night.
wrapped in cold,   late at night.

Give me sum - mer.

Give me sum - mer.

MACHETE

by Richard Hall

MY WEAKNESS

by Richard Hall

NATURAL BLUES

by Richard Hall

Moderato

Oh lor-dy,— trou-ble so hard— oh— lor-dy, trou-ble so hard—

1st time no Drums

don't no-bo-dy know my trou-bles but god——— don't no-bo-dy know my trou-bles but god.—

Oh lor-dy,— trou-ble so hard——— oh— lor-dy,

INSIDE

by Richard Hall

Moderato

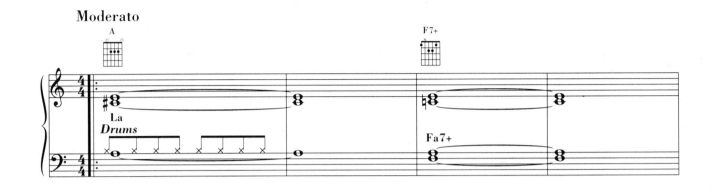

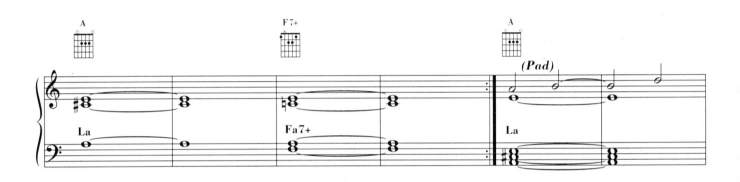

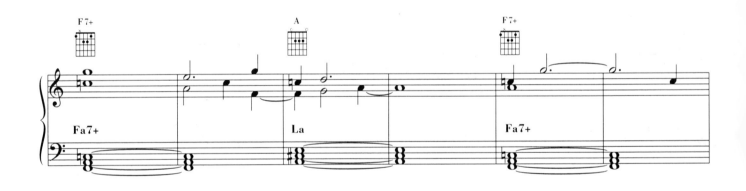

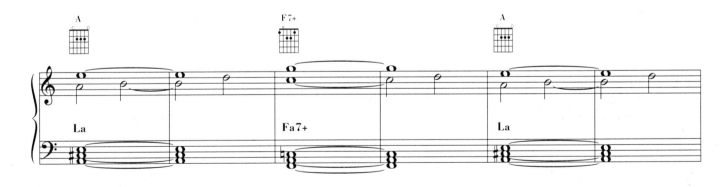

50

PORCELAIN

by Richard Hall

RUN ON

by Richard Hall

repeat fading out

RUSHING

by Richard Hall

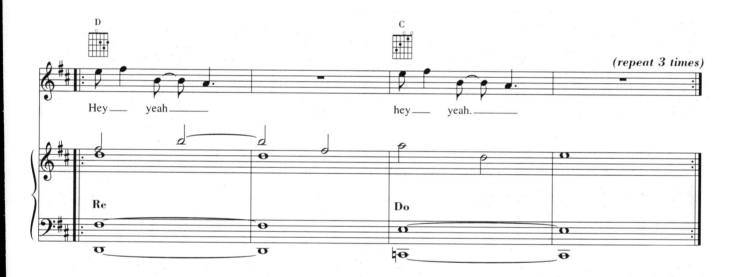

SOUTH SIDE

by Richard Hall

Moderato

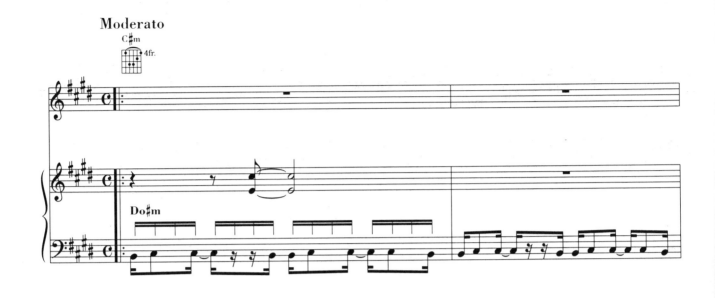

68

THE SKY IS BROKEN

by Richard Hall

See the storm is bro - ken   in the mid-dle of the night   no - thing left here   for me
Wash   it far____   push it out   to sea   there's   no-thing   left here

70

72

WHY DOES MY HEART FEEL SO BAD?

by Richard Hall

INGRAF s.r.l. - Via Monte S. Genesio 7 - Milano
Stampato in Italia - Printed in Italy - Imprimé en Italie 2001